A Beginning-to-Read Book

LIFE SCIENCE

WHAT ANIMALS NEED

by Mary Lindeen

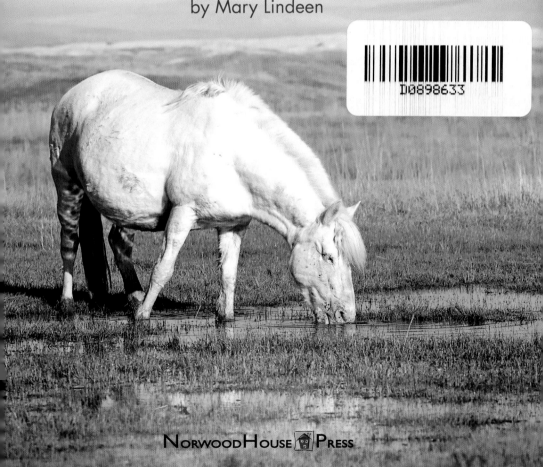

NORWOOD HOUSE PRESS

DEAR CAREGIVER,

The *Beginning to Read—Read and Discover Science* books provide young readers the opportunity to learn about scientific concepts while simultaneously building early reading skills. Each title corresponds to three of the key domains within the Next Generation Science Standards (NGSS): physical sciences, life sciences, and earth and space sciences.

The NGSS include standards that are comprised of three dimensions: Cross-cutting Concepts, Science and Engineering Practices, and Disciplinary Core Ideas. The texts within the *Read and Discover Science* series focus primarily upon the Disciplinary Core Ideas and Cross-cutting Concepts—helping readers view their world through a scientific lens. They pique a young reader's curiosity and encourage them to inquire and explore. The Connecting Concepts section at the back of each book offers resources to continue that exploration. The reinforcement activities at the back of the book support Science and Engineering Practices—to understand how scientists investigate phenomena in that world.

These easy-to-read informational texts make the scientific concepts accessible to young readers and prompt them to consider the role of science in their world. On one hand, these titles can develop background knowledge for exploring new topics. Alternately, they can be used to investigate, explain, and expand the findings of one's own inquiry. As you read with your child, encourage her or him to "observe"—taking notice of the images and information to formulate both questions and responses about what, how, and why something is happening.

Above all, the most important part of the reading experience is to have fun and enjoy it!

Sincerely,

Shannon Cannon

Shannon Cannon, Ph.D.
Literacy Consultant

Norwood House Press
For more information about Norwood House Press please visit our website at www.norwoodhousepress.com or call 866-565-2900.
© 2019 Norwood House Press. Beginning-to-Read™ is a trademark of Norwood House Press. All rights reserved. No part of this book may be reproduced or utilized in any form or by any means without written permission from the publisher.

Editor: Judy Kentor Schmauss

Designer: Lindaanne Donohoe

Photo Credits:
Shutterstock, cover, 1, 3, 4, 5, 6, 7, 9 (inset), 10 (insets), 10-11, 12-13, 14, 15, 16, 17, 18-19, 22-23, 23 (inset), 24-25, 26-27; iStock Photo, 8-9, 20-21

Library of Congress Cataloging-in-Publication Data
Names: Lindeen, Mary, author.
Title: What animals need / by Mary Lindeen.
Description: Chicago, IL : Norwood House Press, [2018] I Series: A beginning to read book I Audience: K to Grade 3.
Identifiers: LCCN 2018004474 (print) I LCCN 2018013277 (ebook) I ISBN 9781684041558 (eBook) I ISBN 9781599538990 (library edition : alk. paper)
Subjects: LCSH: Life (Biology)-Juvenile literature. I Animals-Juvenile literature.
Classification: LCC QH325 (ebook) I LCC QH325 .L6945 2018 (print) I DDC 570-dc23
LC record available at https://lccn.loc.gov/2018004474

Hardcover ISBN: 978-1-59953-899-0   Paperback ISBN: 978-1-68404-146-6

334R-092020
Manufactured in the United States of America in North Mankato, Minnesota.

How are these things alike?
They are all living things.

Living things need air.

People need air.

Animals need air, too.

Did You Know?

Scientists put all living things into two groups: plants and animals. People are definitely not plants! We are a kind of animal.

Living things need water.

People need water.

Animals need water, too.

Animals that need a lot of water have to live in wet places.

But other animals can live in dry places.

Living things need warmth.

People need warmth.

They choose clothes
and homes that
keep them
warm.

Animals also need warmth.

Animals that need a lot of warmth live in hot places.

But other animals can
live in cold places.

Living things need food.

People need food.

Animals need food, too.

Living things need sunlight.

Sunlight keeps Earth warm.

Sunlight also helps plants grow.

People need plants for food.

Animals need plants
for food, too.

Animals can be changed by
the places where they live.

Did You Know?

Dogs and cats are often enemies.
But some dogs and cats learn to
like each other when they live in
the same home.

Animals can also make changes to the places where they live.

air

water

warmth

food

sunlight

CONNECTING CONCEPTS

CLOSE READING OF NONFICTION TEXT

Close reading helps children comprehend text. It includes reading a text, discussing it with others, and answering questions about it. Use these questions to discuss this book with your child:

- How are animals and people alike?
- What do animals that live in hot places need?
- How does the sunlight help animals?
- Name an example of an animal that can change because of the place it lives.
- Name one way an animal can change the place where it lives.

SCIENCE IN THE REAL WORLD

Find pictures of animals and write captions about where they live, what they eat, and so on. Put the pictures together to make an Animal Scrapbook.

SCIENCE AND ACADEMIC LANGUAGE

Make sure your child understands the meaning of the following words:

alike   enemies   groups   scientists

Have him or her use the words in a sentence.

FLUENCY

Help your child practice fluency by using one or more of the following activities:

1. Reread the book to your child at least two times while he or she uses a finger to track each word as it is read.

2. Read a line of the book, then reread it as your child reads along with you.

3. Ask your child to go back through the book and read the words he or she knows.

4. Have your child practice reading the book several times to improve accuracy, rate, and expression.

FOR FURTHER INFORMATION

Books:

Austin, Elizabeth. *What Do Living Things Need?* Huntington Beach, CA: Teacher Created Materials, 2014.

Bové, Jennifer. *Animal Homes (Ranger Rick: Animal Fun for Young Children)*. Guildford, CT: Muddy Boots, 2016.

Kurtz, Kevin. *Living Things and Nonliving Things: A Compare and Contrast Book*. Mt. Pleasant, SC: Arbordale Publishing, 2017.

Websites:

National Geographic Kids: Desert
https://kids.nationalgeographic.com/explore/nature/habitats/desert/#deserts-camel-sahara.jpg

Ranger Rick: Polar Bears: A Life on Ice
https://rangerrick.org/ranger_rick/polar-bears-a-life-on-ice/

Time for Learning: Basic Needs of Animals
https://www.time4learning.com/_swf/demos/childu/12science_basic_needs.html

Word List

What Animals Need uses the 78 words listed below. *High-frequency words* are those words that are used most often in the English language. They are sometimes referred to as sight words because children need to learn to recognize them automatically when they read. *Content words* are any words specific to a particular topic. Regular practice reading these words will enhance your child's ability to read with greater fluency and comprehension.

High-Frequency Words

a	at	for	into	other	the	two
air	be	get	like	people	them	water
all	but	have	look	place(s)	these	we
also	by	help(s)	make	put	they	what
and	can	home(s)	not	same	things	when
are	do	how	of	some	to	where
around	each	in	often	that	too	you

Content Words

alike	clothes	Earth	hot	living	sunlight
animal(s)	cold	enemies	keep(s)	lot	warm
cats	definitely	food	kind	need	warmth
change(d, s)	dogs	groups	learn	plants	wet
choose	dry	grow	live	scientists	

About the Author

Mary Lindeen is a writer, editor, parent, and former elementary school teacher. She has written more than 100 books for children and edited many more. She specializes in early literacy instruction and books for young readers, especially nonfiction.

About the Advisor

Dr. Shannon Cannon is an elementary school teacher in Sacramento, California. She has served as a teacher educator in the School of Education at UC Davis, where she also earned her Ph.D. in Language, Literacy, and Culture. As a member of the clinical faculty, she supervised pre-service teachers and taught elementary methods courses in reading, effective teaching, and teacher action research.